Ketogenic Diet: 21-Day Healthy Ketogenic Diet Meal Plan to Get Lean and Lose Weight Fast as Hell

Tips For Low-Carb Ketogenic Diet Food List, Recipes, Crock Pot, Slow Cooker

KAREN TAYLOR

ISBN-10: 1523385111

ISBN-13: 978-1523385119

CONTENTS

Introduction

Are you struggling with your weight? Do you want to shed pounds without skipping any meals or starving yourself? Are you looking for a safe and effective way to be healthy and lean? Then let me introduce to you a diet that has been changing the lives of millions of people worldwide—the Ketogenic Diet.

According to a study published in 2014 in *The Lancet*, a medical journal, 2.1 billion individuals, almost 30% of the world's total population, are either overweight or obese. In the United States alone, the Center for Disease Control and Prevention reported that almost 70% of the adult population in the country is either obese or overweight. In the past, weight and obesity were only significant issues in high-income countries. However, this latest study showed that these health problems are also prevalent in low-income countries.

Being overweight or obese is considered a health problem because both can put you at a greater risk of developing serious and chronic conditions, such as hypertension, diabetes, stroke, and more.

According to health experts, one major reason why there are billions of overweight and obese people is because most individuals today have diets that are made up of foods rich in sugar, salt, and calories. Avoiding physical activities, skipping the gym, or living a sedentary lifestyle are more factors that contribute to people being obese and overweight.

What I want you to understand is that in addition to cutting off the flabs in your belly and achieving the body you always wanted, your main purpose of going on a diet should also be to become healthy and to avoid the complications that go along with being overweight or obese.

You should be careful of the dozens of weight loss diet fads that are rampant today because most of these will only help you shed off your water weight, which is easily regained when you go back to your old diet. Plus, these lose-weight-fast diets typically include skipping meals or replacing your food with "liquid meals," which is unhealthy and bad for your body. What you want is to follow a healthy diet that still allows you to eat food and lose weight at the same time. One way that you could achieve this is through the Ketogenic Diet, which I will share with you in this book.

Before I move on any further, let me thank you and congratulate you for purchasing this book, "21-Day Healthy Ketogenic Diet Meal Plan to Get Lean and Lose Weight Fast as Hell."

This book is perfect for Ketogenic Diet beginners because I included a chapter that will allow you to learn more about the diet's history, how it works, its benefits, and how it can help you lose weight. There's also a chapter about the Ketogenic Diet food list and recipes that you can include in your 21-day Ketogenic Diet meal plan. Lastly, there is a chapter that contains tips and strategies to help you achieve your health goals through this diet.

Thank you again for purchasing this book. Good luck on your journey to a healthier and leaner you!

Chapter 1: The Ketogenic Diet

The History of the Ketogenic Diet and Why It Works

The Ketogenic Diet is one of the most popular weight loss diet plans, and is followed by millions of individuals worldwide. You may think that Ketogenic Diet is just another fad and has only been around for years, but the Ketogenic Diet was developed nine decades ago.

In 1924, clinician and scientist Dr. Russell M. Wilder of the Mayo Clinic developed the Ketogenic Diet, not to help individuals lose weight, but to help minimize seizures of children who have epilepsy. The Ketogenic Diet became very popular during that decade until the 1940's when anticonvulsant drugs were introduced.

The Ketogenic Diet only gained the spotlight again for epilepsy therapy when Charlie Abrahams, son of Hollywood director Jim Abrahams, was featured on NBC's show, *Dateline*. The show was about his recovery from epileptic seizures through the Ketogenic Diet. Even after visiting several doctors, trying several medications and treatments, and undergoing brain surgery, Charlie still suffered from frequent seizures until his dad discovered a book on Ketogenic Diet. By going through the diet (which was offered by Johns Hopkins Medical Center) for 5 years, starting when he was a toddler, Charlie hadn't experienced seizures ever since.

Charlie's incredible victory over epileptic seizures through the Ketogenic Diet made his family decide to establish the Charlie Foundation. This paved the way to start further studies on the diet, where researchers found that other than controlling epilepsy, the Ketogenic Diet has other health benefits, such as weight loss, better management of type 2 diabetes, and more.

Changing The Way We Diet- Ketogenic Diet Explained

The Ketogenic Diet sounds a little bit intimidating; however, it is very easy to understand. It is simply a diet that is high in fat and low in carbohydrates.

But is a high-fat diet bad for your health? Take note that even though fats will make up most of your meals, these fats should be quality fats, such as olive oil, avocado, and almond oil. Hydrogenated fats, such as margarine, are "unnatural fats" and avoided in this diet plan.

So how can a high-fat diet help you shed fat? Most people have diets that are high in carbohydrates. When you eat pasta, bread, or rice, your body transforms these carbs into glucose and insulin that is used by your body for energy. And since your body is dependent on glucose for energy, fat that is also consumed when you eat food is stored in your body and not burned.

The idea of the Ketogenic Diet is to increase your intake of healthy fats and lower your consumption of carbs in order for your body to enter into a metabolic state called *ketosis*. When your body is in ketosis, it burns the breakdown fats produced by the liver called *ketones*. In short, instead of burning glucose for energy, your body will burn fat; this will help you to lose weight and achieve a leaner body.

There are three types of Ketogenic Diet, the Standard Ketogenic Diet (SKD), which is suitable for people who have sedentary lifestyles; Cyclical Ketogenic Diet (CKD) for individuals who are into sports or bodybuilding; and Targeted Ketogenic Diet (TKD), which is for people who are going trying to begin a regular physical activity.

Although the Ketogenic Diet is proven to be effective in helping you lose weight, you must remember that it takes discipline and careful watch over your diet to be successful in achieving your weight goal. This means you should carefully monitor the calories you consume, as well as the macronutrients (protein, fats, and carbs) that you eat.

While you're on the diet, it's recommended to keep your consumption of carbs to 20-60 grams per day. Ideally, an SKD requires you to have 70%-75% fat, 20%-25% protein, and 5%-10% carbs in your daily calories. However, your nutritional needs will still differ depending on your weight, body fat percentage, physical activity, etc. to maintain your body in ketosis. If you want to be sure, you can use applications such as a _keto calculator_ to help you achieve a state of ketosis.

For beginners, it is advised that you use urine ketone sticks in order to monitor the ketones in your body. This is important because you will know if your body is undergoing ketosis and burning fat through the Ketogenic Diet.

Benefits of Ketogenic Diet on Weight Loss

As I mentioned, the Ketogenic Diet was originally developed to help manage or treat seizures, particularly in children with epilepsy. However, further studies showed that the Ketogenic Diet has other benefits to the body such as:

- **Helps achieve weight loss**- Going through a low-carb diet like the Ketogenic Diet automatically decreases your appetite. Your cravings for sweets will be controlled and you will find yourself having less hunger pangs during the diet.

  Also, it is found that shedding weight is faster on Ketogenic Diet because limiting carbs in your diet allows the kidney to remove the excess sodium, therefore also releasing excess water in your body in the first and second week of the diet.

- **Reduces abdominal fat**- If your goal is to get rid of the fats in your midsection and achieve a flat belly, then the Ketogenic Diet is for you. This food plan has also been seen to reduce abdominal fat, which also known as the "beer belly."

- **Increases levels of good cholesterol**- A low-carb and high-fat diet such as the Ketogenic Diet is proven to be effective in increasing HDL and LDL (also known as good cholesterol) in the blood. Having high levels of good cholesterol in your body decreases your risk of having heart disease.

- **Reduces insulin and blood sugar levels**- When consumed, carbs are broken into glucose therefore increasing the sugar levels in the blood. People who have type 2 diabetes have a hard time managing their blood sugar when they are in high-carb diets. That's why many experts believe that the Ketogenic Diet is advisable for diabetes patients because it helps them manage their blood sugar level well.

  A study in 2005 involving 21 type 2 diabetes patients underwent the Ketogenic Diet for 16 weeks. After the experiment, the results showed that all the patients showed improvements in their blood sugar levels while some were even able to reduce the use of medications for diabetes because of the diet.

- **Reduces cancer cells in the body-** A study at the British Columbia Cancer Research Center on the Ketogenic Diet shows that this low-carb, high-fat diet can significantly control the development of cancer cells in the body. That's because it is believed that cancer cells survive on glucose. And when the supply of glucose is limited from the diet, it is likely that cancer cells will not be able to multiply.

  The Ketogenic Diet is not yet proven to have therapeutic effects on cancer; it is only one of the ways to prevent developing certain types of cancer.

- **Helps prevent brain diseases-** Studies show that when the body is under ketosis, it produces antioxidants that help improve mental health and decreases the risk of developing serious neurological disorders such as Alzheimer's disease, ALS, and Parkinson's disease.

Although the Ketogenic Diet is proven to help you lose weight and provide other health benefits, like the ones mentioned above, it is still best that you consult with your healthcare provider, especially if you have existing health conditions.

Chapter 2: Ketogenic Diet Food List

Although your goal is to lose weight by going on a diet, following the Ketogenic Diet doesn't mean that you will have to skip meals or starve yourself in order to shed pounds. In fact, you don't even have to shop for special type of foods, but can instead stick with foods that are low in carbs and close to their natural state.

Any type of grains (wheat, oats, corn, quinoa, rice), even whole wheat, should be avoided in this diet. Also, any type of food made from grains (baked goods, pastries, etc.), as well as food or beverages that are rich in sugar, should be avoided. Since your aim is to eat all-natural foods as much as possible, processed foods should be avoided as well.

To give you an idea on what foods you should include on your next trip to the grocery store, some types of food that you can consume in the Ketogenic Diet and those you can eat occasionally are listed below.

Ketogenic Diet Delicious Approved Foods

Fats and Oils

Even though fats will make up most of your diet, it doesn't mean that you can consume any fat-rich foods. Remember: you should still stick to good or natural sources of fat. Some good examples are:

Clarified butter/ghee

Coconut oil

Organic butter

Lard

Chicken/duck fat

Fish rich in Omega-3 (salmon, mackerel, trout, tuna, herring)

*Avocado oil

Avocado

Unsweetened peanut butter

*Macadamia oil/nuts

*Organic olive oil

*Flaxseed oil

*Sesame oil

*Not for high heat cooking

Protein

Organic, grass fed, and free-range are your best choices for protein.

Free range eggs

Grass fed meat (beef, pork, veal, lamb, etc.)

Organic or free range poultry (chicken, duck, etc.)

Wild caught fish (salmon, tuna, snapper, trout, halibut, etc.)

Shellfish (lobster, crab, mussels, oysters, clams, etc.)

Bacon and sausages (these are allowed in the diet, however you have to check if the product is cured in sugar, or if there are other fillers added)

Vegetables/Fruits

To achieve ketosis and limit your carb intake it's best to stick with green leafy vegetables (preferably organic) such as:

Spinach

Kale

Lettuce

Collards

Cucumber

*Broccoli

*Cabbage

*Nightshades (eggplant, peppers, tomatoes)

The choice of fruit is very limited in the Ketogenic Diet since these are high in carbs and sugar. What you can only eat in this diet are:

Avocado

*Berries

*Can be eaten occasionally

Dairy Products

When buying dairy products, you should always choose full-fat variants and avoid low-fat or fat-free variants. Some Ketogenic Diet-approved dairy products include:

Full-fat yogurt

Sour cream

Cheeses (mozzarella, cheddar, cream cheese, etc.)

Cottage cheese

Whipped cream/ heavy cream

Spices, Condiments, Etc.

Mayonnaise (preferably homemade)

Mustard (preferably homemade)

Any spices or herbs

*Stevia

*Agave nectar

*Raw honey

*Sugar-free ketchup

*Dark chocolate

*Cocoa

*Can be consumed occasionally

1. **Beverages**

   o Water

   o Black coffee (you can add cream if you want)

   o Herbal tea

   o *Dry red/white wine

   o *Unsweetened spirits (*Can be consumed occasionally)

Chapter 3: 21-Day Delicious Ketogenic Recipes

In order to lose weight and fully achieve the benefits of the

Ketogenic Diet, you must be fully committed to following the diet

plan and what types of food you can include in your diet. It will also

help you a lot if you create a Ketogenic Diet plan at least for two or

three weeks in advance, so you will be prepared on what meals you're

going to eat. Take note that going through this diet also means that

you will have to spend more time in the kitchen. But don't worry;

I've also included some recipes here in this chapter that you can whip up easily using the crock-pot or slow cooker.

21 Easy-Whip Keto Breakfast Recipes

1. Perfect Keto Omelet

Nutritional Value: Calories-203, Fat-5g, Protein-20g, Carbs-18g

Ingredients:

- 4 egg whites

- 1 egg yolk

- 2 tbsp. coconut milk

- 1 medium sized tomat0 (chopped)

- 1 cup spinach (chopped)

- ½ onion (chopped)

- ½ tsp. dried basil

- clarified butter

Procedure:

1. Place the eggs (yolk and whites) and milk in a bowl and whisk together.

2. Drizzle clarified butter on a pan over medium heat and then sauté the tomatoes, spinach, and onion for 4-5 minutes or until the spinach starts to wilt.

3. Place the cooked vegetables on the side and pour the egg mixture on the pan. Cook until firm.

4. Place the egg on a plate and top with cooked vegetables on one half and then fold to make an omelet.

5. Serve.

2. Bacon n' Cheese Omelet

Nutritional Value: Calories-463, Fat-39g, Protein-24g, Carbs-1g

Ingredients:

- 2 cooked bacon strips

- 2 whole eggs (preferably organic)

- 4 tbsp. grated cheddar

- 2 stalks onion chives (chopped)

- 1 tsp. lard or bacon fat

Procedure:

1. Heat lard on a non-stick frying pan over medium fire.

2. Scramble the eggs and pour on the hot pan. Move the pan to cover the edges.

3. While cooking, sprinkle eggs with onion chives and season with salt and pepper.

4. Place the cooked bacon strips at the center and top with cheddar cheese.

5. Fold the egg towards the middle to create an omelet.

3. On-the-Go Raspberry Shake

Nutritional Value: Calories-319, Fat-15g, Protein-28g, Carbs-9g

Ingredients:

- ¾ cups raspberries (frozen)

- 1 scoop protein powder (strawberry flavor)

- 1 cup almond milk

- 1 heaping tbsp. all-natural peanut butter

- ½ tsp. cinnamon powder

- ¼ tsp. ginger

Procedure:

1. Add all ingredients to the blender and mix until smooth.

4. Ham n' Eggs Cups

Nutritional Value: Calories-203, Fat-5g, Protein-20g, Carbs-18g

Ingredients:

- ¼ lb. cooked ham (cubed)

- 6 whole eggs (preferably organic)

- 1 small onion (chopped)

- 1 stalk onion chives (chopped)

- 3 cloves of garlic (minced)

- 1 cup cheddar cheese (shredded)

- ½ cup heavy cream

- 1 tbsp. organic butter

- 3 tbsp. ghee

- salt and pepper to taste

Procedure:

1. Set oven at 400F.

2. Heat ghee on a frying pan over medium fire. Throw in the onions and cook sauté until the onion turns translucent.

3. Add the garlic and cook for another 2 minutes

4. In a bowl, combine all the ingredients including the sautéed garlic and oil except the organic butter. Mix well.

5. Brush five ramekins with the butter and pour in the egg mixture. Fill about ½-3/4 of the ramekin. Cook in the oven for 20 minutes or until the egg turns slightly brown.

5. Breakfast Sausage Patties

Nutritional Value: Calories-655, Fat-56g, Protein-30.5g, Carbs-3.5g

Ingredients:

- 2 oz. sausage patties

- 2 cooked bacon strips

- ¼ cup Monterey Jack cheese (grated)

- 2 whole organic eggs

- ½ tbsp. organic butter

- ½ tbsp. all-natural peanut butter

Procedure:

1. Heat a non-stick skillet over medium fire and lay the sausage patties to cook. Brown on both sides.

2. While cooking the other side of the patty, place the grated cheese on top and cover the pan.

3. Remove the cooked patties from the pan and set aside on a plate.

4. Scramble the eggs and cook it using the same skillet.

5. Lay the cooked scramble egg on top of the patties and then top with the cooked bacon strips.

6. Mix in a small bowl the butter and peanut butter. Scoop on top of the bacon.

7. Serve.

6. Spinach and Ricotta Omelet

Nutritional Value: Calories-620, Fat-56g, Protein-25g, Carbs-5.5g

Ingredients:

- 3 whole organic eggs

- 2 cups spinach (coarsely chopped)

- 1 small onion (cut into strips)

- 1 stalk of chive (chopped)

- 1 oz. ricotta

- 2 tbsp. heavy cream

- 2 tbsp. butter

Procedure:

1. Melt butter in a pan over medium heat.

2. Throw in the onion strips to the pan and cook until it caramelizes.

3. Add the spinach to the pan and cook until the leaves begin to wilt. Season well with salt and pepper. Set aside when cooked.

4. In bowl, whisk the eggs and cream. Season with salt and pepper.

5. Using the same pan, cook the egg mixture over low fire.

6. When the egg is almost done, add the cooked spinach on one side of the egg and top with crumbled ricotta.

7. Fold the egg to make an omelet. Serve with chopped chives for garnish.

7. Chicken Sausages and Cheese Cups

Nutritional Value: Calories-711, Fat-65.3g, Protein-34.3g, Carbs-5.8g

Ingredients:

- 2 pcs. chicken sausage (cut into small cubes)

- 1/2 cup cheddar cheese (grated)

- 5 egg yolks (preferably organic)

- ¼ cup coconut flour

- ½ tsp. rosemary

- a pinch of cayenne pepper

- ¼ tsp. baking soda

- ¼ cup coconut oil

- 2 tbsp. coconut milk

- 2 tsp. lime juice

- salt to taste

Procedure:

1. Set oven at 350F.

2. Place the sausages in a pan over medium fire and cook until brown. Set aside.

3. In a bowl, combine the coconut flour, baking soda, cayenne, and rosemary.

4. Using an electronic hand mixer, whisk the yolks in another bowl for 5 minutes or until it turns thick.

5. Add the lime juice, coconut milk, and coconut oil into the egg and whisk again.

6. Slowly add the coconut flour to the egg mixture and combine well.

7. Fold in the grated cheese into the mixture.

8. Place this mixture into two ramekins filling up to ¾ of the cup. Top with the cooked sausages and bake in the oven for about 20 minutes or until it turns golden brown.

9. Let it cool into room temperature before serving.

8. Cheese and Bacon Bites

Nutritional Value: Calories-531, Fat-51.3g, Protein-32.7g, Carbs-4.7g

Ingredients:

- 1 cup grated cheddar cheese

- 3 bacon strips (chopped)

- 3 whole organic eggs

- 3 tbsp. all-natural/organic salsa

- a pinch of paprika

- a pinch of cayenne pepper

- salt and pepper to taste

Procedure:

1. Preheat oven to 400F.

2. Divide the cheese into three piles and lay them on a greased baking sheet.

3. Season the cheese piles with paprika, cayenne, salt, and pepper and place in the oven to cook for 12 minutes.

4. Cook the bacon strips until crisp while waiting for the cheese.

5. Immediately remove the melted cheese on the baking sheet and transfer into three different small bowls to create a bowl shape.

6. Remove the cooked bacon from the pan and use the bacon fat to cook the eggs. You may want to use a mold (circular) while frying the eggs to keep a perfect shape.

7. When the eggs are cooked, place it on top of the cheese cups, and top it with crispy bacon and a scoop of salsa.

8. Serve.

9. Cast Iron Breakfast Plate

Nutritional Value: Calories-203, Fat-5g, Protein-20g, Carbs-18g

Ingredients:

- 3 chicken sausages (sliced thin)

- 2 cups Portobello mushrooms (chopped)

- 3 cups spinach (roughly chopped)

- 1 ½ cup grated cheddar cheese

- 10 whole organic eggs

- 1 tbsp. ranch dressing

- 2 tsp. Sriracha sauce

- salt and pepper to taste

Procedure:

1. Set the oven to 400F.

2. Heat the cast iron skillet over medium-high fire. Add the sausages when the pan is hot.

3. Throw in the spinach and mushrooms when you're ready to flip the sausage slices. Season with salt and pepper.

4. In a bowl, scramble the eggs and then add the ranch dressing and Sriracha sauce.

5. Once the spinach is cooked, add the grated cheese on top and then pour the egg mixture in the skillet. Season with salt and pepper.

6. Turn of the fire and place the skillet in the oven to cook for 10 minutes and then broil for 4 minutes.

7. Remove from the oven and let it cool before serving.

10. Choco-Berry Chia Pudding

Nutritional Value: Calories-235, Fat-12g, Protein-30g, Carbs-19g

Ingredients:

- 3 tbsp. chia seeds

- 1 heaping tbsp. cacao powder

- 1 cup almond milk (unsweetened)

- ¼ cup frozen raspberry

- 1 tsp. agave nectar

Procedure:

1. In a bowl mix the almond milk and the cacao power.

2. Add the chia seeds and mix. Let it sit for 5 minutes.

3. Mix the chia seed mixture and then leave for another 30 minutes in the fridge.

4. Add raspberries and drizzle with agave nectar on top before serving.

11. Creamy Pesto Eggs

Nutritional Value: Calories-467, Fat-41.5g, Protein-20.4g, Carbs-3.3g

Ingredients:

- 3 whole organic eggs

- 1 tbsp. pesto sauce

- 1 tbsp. clarified butter

- 2 tbsp. sour cream

- salt and pepper to taste

Procedure:

1. Put the eggs in a bowl and whisk. Season with salt and pepper.

2. Place a non-stick skillet on low fire and pour the egg mixture. Add the clarified butter in the pan and constantly whisk until you achieve a creamy texture.

3. Add the pesto to the egg and mix well.

4. Turn off the heat and then add the sour cream and mix again.

5. Serve with avocado on the side.

12.   Keto Breakfast Salad

Nutritional Value: Calories-422, Fat-35.5g, Protein-17.4g, Carbs-6.6g

Ingredients:

- 1 tbsp. clarified butter

- 1 whole organic egg

- 2 bacon strips (chopped)

- 1 small zucchini (diced into small pieces)

- 1 clove of garlic (chopped)

- 1 stalk chives (chopped)

- salt and pepper to taste

Procedure:

1. Drizzle the clarified butter on a non-stick skillet and heat over medium fire.

2. Sauté the garlic until lightly brown and then add the bacon. Cook until the bacon turns brown.

3. Throw in the zucchini to the pan and cook for about 12-15 minutes. Season with salt and pepper.

4. Place the cooked zucchini on a plate and garnish with chopped chives.

5. Fry the egg (sunny side up) on the pan. When cooked placed on top of the zucchini salad.

6. Serve warm.

13. Easy Egg Salad

Nutritional Value: Calories-166, Fat-14g, Protein-10g, Carbs-.85g

Ingredients:

- 6 medium-sized organic eggs

- 1 tsp. mustard

- 2 tbsp. mayonnaise

- 1 tsp. lime juice

- a pink of paprika

- salt and pepper to taste

- *lettuce

- *cooked bacon strips

*(*Not included in nutritional value)*

Procedure:

1. Boil the eggs in a saucepan for about 10 minutes. Remove the eggs from the heat and let it cool down with running water.

2. Peel the eggs and coarsely chop with knife or using a food processor.

3. Add the mayonnaise, mustard, lime juice, paprika, salt and pepper.

4. Mix until all ingredients are well combined.

5. Serve on top of lettuce and garnish with chopped bacon strips.

14. Pumpkin and Sausage Scramble

Nutritional Value: Calories-577, Fat-47.3g, Protein-30.7g, Carbs-6.1g

Ingredients:

- 250g sausage (casing removed)

- 1 cup pumpkin (diced)

- 3 organic eggs

- 1 cup cheddar cheese (grated)

- 2 garlic cloves (chopped)

- 1 small onion (chopped)

- ¼ cup heavy cream

- ½ tbsp. mustard

- 2 tbsp. lard

- salt and pepper to taste

Procedure:

1. Set oven at 350F

2. Place a skillet on medium-high heat and grease with 1 tbsp. of lard. Place the sausages breaking it into smaller pieces. Cook for about 8 minutes or until brown.

3. When cooked, place the sausages on a baking tray and set aside.

4. Using the same pan, grease the pan with the remaining lard and sauté the onion and garlic for about 5-7 minutes; or until the onions caramelize.

5. Throw in the diced pumpkin into the pan with the onion and garlic and cook until tender.

6. When cooked, add the pumpkin with the sausage. Add the mustard, grated cheddar (set aside ¼ for topping) and mix well.

7. In a separate bowl, whisk the eggs with the cream and season with salt and pepper.

8. Pour the egg mixture over the sausage and pumpkin and top with the remaining cheese.

9. Place in the over to cook for 25 minutes or until it turns golden brown.

10. Let it cool for a few minutes before serving.

15. Low-Carb Mixed Berry Shake

Nutritional Value: Calories-400, Fat-37.7g, Protein-4g, Carbs-7g

Ingredients:

- ¼ cup frozen blueberries

- ¼ cup strawberries (sliced)

- 1/3 cup coconut cream

- 1 tbsp. extra virgin olive oil

- ½ cup almond milk

- 3-4 ice cubes

Procedure:

1. Add all the ingredients in a blender and mix until you achieve a smooth consistency.

16. Avocado and Egg Salad

Nutritional Value: Calories-616, Fat-56.8g, Protein-16.5g, Carbs-4.8g

<u>Ingredients:</u>

- 4 whole organic eggs

- 1 large avocado (cut in half and pitted)

- 2 tbsp. cream cheese

- 1 tsp. mustard

- ¼ cup organic mayonnaise

- 2 scallions (chopped)

- salt and pepper to taste

<u>Procedure:</u>

1. Boil the eggs in water for 10 minutes. When cooked, run the eggs on run water before peeling.

2. Peel the eggs and coarsely chop.

3. In a medium-sized bowl, mix the eggs, chopped scallions, mayo, cream cheese, and mustard. Combine well and season with salt and pepper.

4. Scoop the avocado flesh leaving at least ½ in. of flesh. Add the avocado flesh in the egg mixture and combine well.

5. Finally, scoop enough amounts of the egg and avocado salad in the avocado cups. Serve.

17. Complete Breakfast Plate

Nutritional Value: Calories-489, Fat-41.3g, Protein-19.5g, Carbs-6.6g

Ingredients:

- 5 bacon strips (cooked)

- 2 Portobello mushrooms or 2 cups of spinach

- 1 small avocado (pitted and chopped)

- 1 whole organic egg

- 1 tbsp. clarified butter

- salt and pepper to taste

Procedure:

1. Heat the clarified butter on a pan over low heat. Cook the mushrooms in the pan for at least 5 minutes and season with salt and pepper.

2. On a separate pan, cook the bacon until crisp and followed by the egg.

3. Serve the cooked bacon, egg, and mushrooms on a plate with the chopped avocado.

18. The Green Breakfast Plate

Nutritional Value: Calories-360, Fat-29.3g, Protein-17.6g, Carbs-4.3g

Ingredients:

- 2 whole organic eggs

- 1 green bell pepper (cut into rings, you'll only need 2 pcs.)

- 1 cup spinach (roughly chopped)

- 1 small onion (chopped)

- 3 cooked bacon strips (chopped)

- 1 tbsp. butter (unsalted)

- salt and pepper to taste

Procedure:

1. Heat a non-stick pan over low fire. Place the two bell pepper rings on the pan and crack one egg each in the rings. Season with salt and pepper and cook until the eggs are firm.

2. In another pan, melt the butter on medium fire and sauté the chopped onion until it caramelizes.

3. Add the spinach to the pan and cook until wilted. Add the chopped bacon to the pan and cook for another 1-2 minutes.

4. Serve the eggs and bell pepper with the spinach on a plate.

19. Keto Approved Pancakes

Nutritional Value: Calories-443, Fat-46g, Protein-12g, Carbs-5g

<u>Ingredients:</u>

- 1 cup CarbQuick Baking Mix

- ½ tsp. baking soda

- 1 small organic egg

- ¼ cup water

- ½ cup heavy cream

- ½ stick butter (unsalted)

- 1 tbsp. vanilla syrup (sugar free)

- 6 cooked bacon strips (chopped)

<u>Procedure:</u>

1. Melt the butter in a pan or in the microwave for a few seconds.

2. In a mixing bowl, combine the baking mix and baking soda.

3. Add the egg, water, heavy cream, melted butter, and vanilla syrup to the bowl and mix well.

4. Heat a non-stick pan over medium-high fire greased with butter.

5. Place a scoop of the pancake batter in the hot pan and place chopped bacon strips on top.

6. Flip the pancake when bubbles start to appear.

7. Cook the other side for 1-2 minutes. Serve warm.

20. Filling Berry Pudding

Nutritional Value: Calories-206, Fat-14.4g, Protein-4.6g, Carbs-20.3g

Ingredients:

- 1 cup full-fat coconut milk

- ¼ cup chia seeds

- ½ tbsp. raw honey

- ½ tbsp. mixed berries

Procedure:

1. In a jar, mix the chia seeds, coconut milk and honey the night before. Leave in the fridge to chill overnight.

2. Top with you choice of berries before consuming for breakfast.

21. Scrambled Egg Delight

Nutritional Value: Calories-227, Fat-16g, Protein-14g, Carbs-3g

Ingredients:

- 5 whole organic eggs

- 8 oz. ham (diced)

- ½ cup cheddar cheese (grated)

- 5 tbsp. heavy cream

- 5 tbsp. water

- 1 stalk green onion (chopped)

- 1 medium tomato (chopped)

- a pinch of garlic powder

- a pinch of onion powder

- salt and pepper to taste

Procedure:

1. Set oven at 450F.

2. In a bowl scramble the eggs with the heavy cream, water, garlic and onion powder. Season with salt and pepper.

3. Pour the egg mixture in a large baking sheet greased with butter and place in the oven to cook for 7-8 minutes.

4. Remove from the oven and then top with the diced ham, green onion, tomato, and cheese.

5. Place back in the oven to cook for about 2-3 minutes or until the cheese melts.

6. Set aside to cool for 5-8 minutes.

7. Scramble the cooked egg and serve in bowls.

21 Delicious Ketogenic Diet Lunch and Dinner

Recipes

1. Keto Fritata

Nutritional Value: Calories-503, Fat-37.5g, Protein-25.5g, Carbs-6.3g

Ingredients:

- 5 whole organic eggs

- 50g bacon

- 10 pcs. asparagus

- 1 small red onion (chopped)

- 1 small red bell pepper (cut into strips)

- 2 tsps. chives (chopped)

- 1 tbsp. parsley (chopped)

- 1 tsp. dried tarragon

- 30ml heavy cream

- 75g ricotta

- 1 tbsp. clarified butter

- salt and pepper to taste

Procedure:

1. Set the oven at 400F.

2. Heat the clarified butter on a pan over medium heat. When the pan is hot, throw in the asparagus and bell pepper, add salt to taste, and cook for about 5 minutes. Set aside.

3. Place the eggs in a large bowl and whisk it with the tarragon, parsley, chives, and cream. Season with salt and pepper.

4. Pour the egg mixture into a baking dish and then also add the cooked veggies and ricotta. Cook for 20 minutes.

5. After the frittata turns firm, lay the bacon strips on top of the egg. Turn down the oven's temperature to 350F and then bake for another 20 minutes.

6. Let the frittata cool for a few minutes before serving.

2. Avocado and Salmon Salad

Nutritional Value: Calories-463, Fat-34.6g, Protein-27g, Carbs-6.4g

Ingredients:

- 1 large avocado (cut into half and pitted)

- 2 pcs. salmon fillet (small)

- 1 shallot (diced)

- ¼ cup organic mayonnaise

- 2 tbsp. lemon juice

- 1 tbsp. fresh dill (chopped)

- 1 tbsp. clarified butter

- salt and pepper to taste

Procedure:

1. Set the oven at 400F.

2. Lay the salmon fillets on a baking sheet and drizzle it with clarified butter and lemon juice. Season with salt and pepper. Place in the oven and cook for 20 minutes.

3. After cooking, let the salmon cool for a few minutes before shredding the meat using a fork.

4. Place the shredded salmon in a bowl and mix with the diced shallot.

5. Add the mayonnaise and dill also in the bowl and mix well. Season with salt and pepper.

6. Scoop the insides of the avocado leaving at least 3cm of flesh with the skin.

7. Mix the scooped avocados with the salmon and combine well.

8. Scoop the salmon and avocado salad into the avocado cups and serve.

3. Vegetarian Keto Salad

Nutritional Value: Calories-436, Fat-36.3g, Protein-17g, Carbs-6.1g

Ingredients:

- 3 pcs. whole organic eggs

- 1 small avocado (sliced)

- cups lettuce (roughly chopped)

- 4 cups arugula (roughly chopped)

- ¼ cup organic mayonnaise

- 2 tsp. mustard

- 2 cloves of garlic (crushed)

- salt and pepper to taste

Procedure:

1. Boil the eggs in a saucepan for 10 minutes. When cooked, place the eggs on running water before peeling. Slice eggs.

2. In a bowl, mix the mayonnaise, mustard, and garlic. Season with salt and pepper; combine well.

3. Place the arugula in a bowl and mix together with the dressing.

4. Top with sliced avocado and eggs before serving.

4. Keto Friendly Chicken Sandwich

Nutritional Value: Calories-772, Fat-56.5g, Protein-44g, Carbs-8g

Ingredients:

For Keto Bread

- 3 organic eggs

- ¼ cup cream cheese

- 1/8 tsp. cream of tartar

- ¼ tsp. salt

For Chicken Spread

- 1 pc. chicken fillet (cubed)

- 2 bacon strips (cut into smaller pieces)

- ½ cup avocado (mashed)

- 2 slices Monterey Jack cheese

- 1 small tomato (sliced)

- 1 tbsp. mayonnaise

- chili flakes to add flavor

- salt and pepper to taste

Procedure:

1. Prepare the bread first. Set oven at 300F.

2. Separate the yolks from the egg whites and place them in two different bowls.

3. Take the bowl with egg whites and add the cream of tartar and salt to it. Using a hand held mixer, whip the eggs and tartar until it turns a little bit stiff.

4. Take the other bowl with the yolks and whip together the cream cheese.

5. Gradually fold in the egg white mixture with the yolk and cream cheese.

6. Lay parchment paper on a baking sheet and scoop ¼ of the batter on the tray and cook in the oven for 25 minutes.

7. While waiting for the keto bread to cook, heat a pan over medium fire. Cook the bacon first followed by chicken cubes using the bacon fat as oil. Season the chicken with salt and pepper. Set aside.

8. When the keto bread is cooked, allow it to cool down a few minutes first before making your sandwich.

9. In a small bowl, combine the mayonnaise and chili flakes together. Use this mixture to spread on top of a keto bread.

10. Add the chicken on top, followed by the bacon strips, cheese, tomato slices, and finally, the mashed avocado. Sandwich with another piece of the keto bread. Serve.

5.   **Bacon Cheese Dog**

Nutritional Value: Calories-379.7, Fat-34.5g, Protein-16.8g, Carbs-0.3g

Ingredients:

- 3 all-natural hot dogs

- 3 strips of quick melt cheese

- 6 bacon strips

- a pinch of garlic powder

- a pinch of onion powder

- salt and pepper to taste

Procedure:

1.   Set the oven at 400F.

2.   Cut slits to the hotdog creating pockets for the cheese. Place the cheese strips inside the hotdog slits.

3. Take the bacon strips and wrap it around the hotdog. Use two bacon strips per hotdog. Secure the bacon with a toothpick.

4. Lay the hotdog on a baking sheet lined with foil or parchment paper and season with onion powder, garlic powder, salt and pepper.

5. Cook in the oven for 40 minutes or until the bacon turns golden brown.

6. Serve with green salad on the side.

6. Zesty Meatballs

Nutritional Value: Calories-339, Fat-23.3g, Protein-32.7g, Carbs-6.2g

Ingredients:

- 16 oz. ground chicken

- ¾ cup grated cheddar

- 2 pcs. scallions (chopped)

- 2 tbsp. cilantro (chopped)

- 1 small red bell pepper (chopped)

- 2 tbsp. flaxseed meal

- 2 tbsp. almond flour

- a pinch of chili flakes

- ½ tsp. garlic powder

- salt and pepper to taste

- 4 tbsp. lemon juice

- ½ tsp. lemon zest

Procedure:

1. Set the oven at 350F.

2. In a bowl, combine the chicken, cheese, red bell pepper, scallions, and cilantro. Season with garlic powder, chili flakes, salt and pepper.

3. Also add in the mixture the lemon juice, zest, almond flour, and flaxseed meal. Combine all the ingredients well using your hands.

4. Roll the mixture into meatballs, about 2 inches in diameter.

5. Place them on a baking tray lined with aluminum foil and bake in the oven for 18-20 minutes.

6. Serve these meatballs with mashed avocado (seasoned with salt, pepper, and lemon juice) on the side.

7.   Spiced Chicken Soup

Nutritional Value: Calories-523, Fat-44.2g, Protein-20.8g, Carbs-3.4g

Ingredients:

- 20 oz. boneless and skinless chicken

- 3 cups beef stock (preferably homemade)

- ¼ cup butter

- 4 tbsp. hot sauce

- salt and pepper to taste

- 1 tsp. onion powder

- 1 tsp. garlic powder

- 1 cup heavy cream

- ¼ cup cream cheese

- ¼ tsp. Xanthan Gum

Procedure:

1. Place all the ingredients except the last three ingredients on the list in a crockpot. Set the heat to high and cook for about 3.5 hours.

2. After cooking, remove the chicken from the pot and place on plate. Shred the chicken using a fork and set aside.

3. Add the remaining ingredients to the crockpot and blend until all the ingredients are well combined.

4. Place the shredded chicken back to the pot mix and serve while hot.

8.   Bacon and Cheese Puff in a Jiffy

Nutritional Value: Calories-227, Fat-16g, Protein-14g, Carbs-3g

Ingredients:

- 1 organic egg

- 2 tbsp. organic butter (at room temperature)

- 3 tbsp. almond flour

- ½ tsp. baking powder

- 2 bacon strips (cooked, chopped)

- 2 tbsps. cheese (shredded)

- 1 stalk of onion leeks (chopped)

- ¼ tsp. Italian spice mix

- salt to taste

Procedure:

1. Place all the ingredients in a mug or a bowl. Mix well.

2. Cook in the microwave set on high for 1 minute and 10 seconds.

3. Let the puff cool down for a few minutes before consuming straight from the mug.

9.   Pan-Seared Asian Salmon

Nutritional Value: Calories-370, Fat-23.5g, Protein-33g, Carbs-2.5g

Ingredients:

- 1 80z. salmon fillet

- 1 tsp. ginger (minced)

- 2 cloves of garlic (minced)

- 1 tbsp. rice vinegar

- 2 tbsp. low-sodium soy sauce

- 1 tbsp. low-sodium fish sauce

- 1 tbsp. keto-friendly ketchup (sugar-free)

- 2 tbsp. white wine

- 2 tbsp. sesame oil

- sesame seeds for garnish

Procedure:

1. In a bowl, mix the soy sauce, fish sauce, ginger, garlic, and rice vinegar. Use this mixture as a marinade to the salmon fillet and let it sit for at least 15 minutes.

2. After 15 minutes, heat a pan greased with sesame oil over medium-high fire and cook the salmon skin side down. Cook for 4 minutes.

3. Flip the fillet to the other side and the pour the marinade over the pan. Cook for another 4 minutes.

4. Remove the fish from the pan and place on a plate. While the marinade is simmering, add the ketchup and white wine in the pan and let it cook for 5 minutes.

5. Serve the salmon fillet garnished with sesame seeds with the sauce on the side.

10.   Homemade Chicken Nuggets

Nutritional Value: Calories-612.5, Fat-50, Protein-38.8g, Carbs-6.8g

Ingredients:

For the Nuggets

- 1.5kg chicken thighs (deboned and skin removed)

- 40g pork rind

- ¼ cup flaxseed meal

- ¼ cup almond meal

- ¼ tsp. paprika

- ¼ tsp. chili powder

- salt and pepper to taste

- a dash of onion powder, garlic powder, and cayenne

- ½ tsp. lime zest

- 1 organic egg

For the Dip

- 1 small avocado

- ½ cup mayonnaise

- 1 tbsp. lime juice

- a pinch of chili flakes and cumin

- a dash of garlic powder

Procedure:

1. Set the oven at 400F.

2. Pat dry the chicken using a paper towel and cut them into nugget size cubes.

3. Using a food processor, mix the pork rind, flaxseed meal, almond meal, zest, paprika, cayenne chili, onion, and garlic powder. Pulse until the ingredients are well combined. Transfer the mixture into a bowl.

4. Scramble the egg in a separate bowl. Then dip the chicken nuggets in the eggs and then into the dry mixture. Make sure that the chicken is coated well.

5. Place the nuggets on a baking tray lined with foil greased with oil.

6. Bake in the oven and cook for 18-20 minutes, or until the chicken is cooked.

7. While waiting for the nuggets to cook, puree and combine all the ingredients of the dip in a blender.

8. Let the nuggets cool for a few minutes before serving with the dip on the side.

11.   **Crock Pot Breadless Pizza**

Nutritional Value: Calories-487, Fat-37g, Protein-30g, Carbs-7.6g

Ingredients:

- 12 oz. ground beef (cooked)

- 12 oz. Italian sausage (cooked)

- 15 oz. low-sodium pizza sauce

- 3 cups shredded mozzarella

- 3 cups baby spinach

- Pepperoni slices

- 1 cup mushroom slices

- 1 cup black olives (sliced)

- 1 small green bell pepper (chopped)

- 1 small white onion (chopped)

- ½ tsp. garlic (minced)

Procedure:

1. In a bowl, combine the ground beef, sausage, and onions.

2. Place half of the meat mixture into a crock pot and then top with ½ of all the pizza toppings. And then repeat the layers; finally topping with the remaining mozzarella cheese.

3. Cook on low for 5-6 hours. Let it cool for a few minutes before serving.

12.   Slow-Cooked Leg of Lamb

Nutritional Value: Calories-574, Fat-38.4g, Protein-46.5g, Carbs-6.1g

Ingredients:

- 2 kg. leg of lamb

- ¼ cup sherry vinegar

- ¼ cup balsamic vinegar

- 2 cups water

- 4 cloves of garlic (chopped)

- 1 sprig rosemary

- salt and pepper to taste

Procedure:

1. Set the oven at 300F.

2. Place the leg of lamb into a baking dish and pour in the water, sherry and balsamic vinegar. Add the garlic and

rosemary sprig in the dish too. Season with salt and pepper, cover and then cook for 2 hours.

3. Remove the cover after 2 hours and then cook again for another 40 minutes.

4. Let the lamb cool for a bit before shredding the meat using a fork.

5. Serve with green leafy salad on the side.

13. Left-Over Lettuce Wraps

Nutritional Value: Calories-338, Fat-25.6g, Protein-23.7g, Carbs-2.4g

Ingredients:

- 2 cups left over slow-cooked leg of lamb

- 1 small red bell pepper (sliced into strips)

- 1 small onion (sliced into strips)

- 6 pcs lettuce

- 2 tsp. garlic paste

- chili flakes

Procedure:

1. Lay the lettuces on a plate and top with the shredded left over leg of lamb.

2. Top with the red bell pepper and onion strip, drizzle with garlic paste and carefully make rolls.

3. Season with chili flakes before consuming.

14. Easy Chicken Patties

Nutritional Value: Calories-159, Fat-11.5g, Protein-9.9g, Carbs-1.7g

Ingredients:

- 12 oz. chicken breast (boiled and cut into chunks)

- 4 bacon strips (cooked)

- 1 large yellow bell pepper

- ¼ cup shredded parmesan cheese

- ¼ cup sun dried tomato paste

- 1 organic egg

- 3 tbsp. almond flour

Procedure:

1. Place the bell pepper into a food processor and pulse until it's finely chopped. Place the chopped pepper into a bowl and dry the excess liquid using a paper towel.

2. Meanwhile, place the cooked chicken and bacon into the food processor. Blend the two together until they turn paste-like.

3. Add the meat mixture with the pepper and combine it with the sundried tomato paste, parmesan, and egg. Mix well.

4. Add the almond flour and mix again.

5. Using your hands, form small patties about 2.5 inches in diameter.

6. Heat a pan greased with clarified butter over medium-high fire and cook the patties until they are crisp.

7. Serve.

15. Spiced Pork Chops

Nutritional Value: Calories-439, Fat-23.7g, Protein-50.3g, Carbs-4.3g

Ingredients:

- 24 oz. pork chop

- 2 tsp. cumin seeds

- 1 tsp. cardamom

- 1 tsp. coriander

- ¼ cup flax seed meal

- salt and pepper to taste

- 3 tbsp. ghee

Procedure:

1. In a bowl, combine the cumin, cardamom, coriander, and flax seed meal.

2. Season the pork chops with salt and pepper and generously coat all sides with the spiced mixture.

3. Heat the ghee on a pan over medium-high fire and place the pork chops to cook once the oil is hot. Cook the pork chops until each side is golden brown.

4. Slice the pork chops and serve with sautéed bell peppers, onions, and celery on the side.

16. Breadless Bacon Burger Patties

Nutritional Value: Calories-227, Fat-16g, Protein-14g, Carbs-3g

Ingredients:

- 28 0z. ground beef (preferably organic)

- 8 bacon strips (chopped)

- ¼ cup shredded cheese

- 2 cloves of garlic (minced)

- 2 tbsp. green onion (chopped)

- 2 tsp. crushed pepper

- 1 ¼ tsp. salt

- 1 tsp. onion powder

- 1 tbsp. low-sodium soy sauce

- 1 tsp. Worcestershire sauce

Procedure:

1. Place a hot iron skillet over medium fire and cook the bacon slices. Once cooked, remove the bacon from the skillet and set aside.

2. Place the ground beef in a large bowl and combine it with ¾ of the cooked bacon and mix it with all of the remaining ingredients. Mix well with your hands.

3. Cook the patties using the same skillet with the bacon fat. Fry for about 4-5 minutes each side.

4. Serve with the remaining bacon on top.

17. Classic Roasted Beef

Nutritional Value: Calories-681, Fat-46.6g, Protein-90g, Carbs-0.3g

Ingredients:

- 40oz. beef ribs

- 2 tsp. garlic powder

- 1 tsp. salt and pepper to taste

Procedure:

1. Place the rib in a baking pan lined with foil and let it sit for an hour in room temperature.

2. Set oven at 375F.

3. In a small bowl, combine the garlic powder, salt, and pepper.

4. Generously rub the seasoning on top of the beef. Cover with foil and place in the oven to cook for an hour.

5. Turn off the heat and let it sit inside the oven for 3 hours without opening the oven.

6. Set the oven back at 375F and then cook for another 40 minutes.

7. Slice the beef and serve with boiled broccoli with ranch dressing on the side.

18.   Slow-Cooked Spiced Beef

Nutritional Value: Calories-223, Fat-5g, Protein-38g, Carbs-5g

Ingredients:

- 16 oz. beef roast

- 3 tbsp. garlic (minced)

- 1 medium-sized onion (chopped)

- 1 tbsp. Italian seasoning

- 2 cups homemade beef broth

- ½ cup red wine

- ½ tsp. chili flakes

- salt and pepper to taste

Procedure:

1. Season the beef roast with salt and pepper.

2. Place in a slow cooker along with the other ingredients and cook under low for 8 hours.

3. Serve with roasted onions and bell pepper slices.

19. Tuna and Avocado Bombs

Nutritional Value: Calories-135, Fat-11.8g, Protein-6.2g, Carbs-0.8g

Ingredients:

- 1 can tuna chunks in water (drained)

- ¼ cup grated parmesan cheese

- ¼ cup organic mayonnaise

- 1 large avocado (cut in cubes)

- 1/3 cup almond flour

- ¼ tsp. onion powder, garlic powder

- salt and pepper to taste

- ½ cup clarified butter

Procedure:

1. Place the drained tuna chunks in a large bowl. Mix in the cheese and mayo and combine well.

2. Carefully fold in the avocado chunks to the tuna and season with onion and garlic powder salt, and pepper.

3. Using your hands, create small balls of the tuna and avocado mixture and roll it on the almond flour.

4. Heat the butter on a pan over medium fire and then fry the tuna and avocado bombs when the butter is hot.

5. Fry for a 5 minutes or until the balls turn golden brown.

20. Keto Green Salad in Vinaigrette

Nutritional Value: Calories-478, Fat-37.3g, Protein-17.1g, Carbs-4.3g

Ingredients:

For the dressing:

- ½ cup raspberries

- ½ cup olive oil

- ½ cup white wine vinegar

- 2 tbsp. agave syrup

For the salad:

- 2 oz. lettuce, kale, and arugula

- 2 cooked bacon strips (chopped)

- 2 tbsp. parmesan cheese

- 2 tbsp. roasted pine nuts

Procedure:

1. Prepare the vinaigrette first by blending all the ingredients and straining out any solids before transferring it in a container.

2. Place the greens in a container with a lid. Pour just enough vinaigrette on the greens, cover and shake well. Place in the fridge the excess vinaigrette, which you can use on your next salad.

3. Top the salad with the chopped bacon strips, pine nuts, and cheese. Serve.

21.   12-Spice Chicken

Nutritional Value: Calories-227, Fat-19.9g, Protein-21.1g, Carbs-0.6g

Ingredients:

For the dry rub:

- 1 tsp. each: ground cumin, paprika, and garlic powder

- ½ tsp. each: cayenne, chili powder, all spice, ground coriander

- ¼ tsp. each: ground cinnamon, ginger powder, ground cardamom

- 1 ½ tsp. salt

- 2 tsp. yellow curry

- 2 kg. chicken thighs

- ¼ cup clarified butter

Procedure:

1.   Set oven at 425F.

2.   Get a bowl and mix all the 12 spices together.

3.   Place the chicken thighs on a baking sheet lined with foil.

4.   Brush the chicken with the clarified butter and then generously rub it with the mixed spices.

5.   Place in the oven to bake for 50 minutes.

6.   Allow to cool for a few minutes before serving.

Chapter 4: Ketogenic Diet Tips for Beginners

I'm sure that you're excited to start the Ketogenic Diet, but let me remind you that it takes dedication and keeping a careful watch on your diet to gain the benefits of this food plan. To help you fully achieve your goals, let me leave you with a few tips in order to be successful in your weight loss journey.

- **Sweep Your Pantry**—Temptation will be hard to resist, especially if you're just starting with the diet. In order to lessen your urges to grab another sugar-rich or carb-rich food, I recommend that you sweep your pantry of any foods that are not Keto friendly. Take this opportunity to re-stock your cupboards with foods that are included in the Ketogenic Diet food list.

- **Count Your Carbs**— Since one of your goals in the Ketogenic Diet is to limit the consumption of carbs, you will have to monitor the number of carbs you eat every meal. This may sound tedious, but with the technology available you can simply log in your meals in a carb counter app like Daily Carb or Carbs Control to track your carb intake.

- **Choose All Natural**— The Ketogenic Diet isn't a meal plan that requires you to only consume special foods. However, you only must consume foods that are closest to their natural state. Avoid foods that are processed or contain artificial flavors; instead, choose foods that are fresh, organic, or homemade.

- **Plan Your Meals**—In order to achieve a state of ketosis (which is the goal of the diet), you have to have control over the food you eat. In order to do this, it's best that you plan your meals ahead of time so that you know what to prepare beforehand.

Speaking of preparing meals, expect that you will be spending more time in the kitchen than before because most keto meals are prepared from scratch. However, if you don't have the luxury of time, you can prepare your meals ahead for the week and then store them in the fridge after so you can just re-heat when you're ready to eat them.

- **Drink Loads of Water**— One of the effects of the Ketogenic Diet is to flush out the excess water in your body. Although this is good, you also have to make sure that you are always well hydrated. It's a good rule drink at least eight glasses of water every day to ensure that you have enough H2O in your body.

- **Use Ketone Strips**— If you're a beginner, it would be very tricky to track if your body is undergoing ketosis. That's why it's recommended to use ketone strips like the Ketostix

Reagent Strips in order to monitor your body's metabolic state.

Follow these tips and use the recipes I shared with you in the previous chapter, and you'll see yourself shedding weight fast as hell!

Keto Breakfast for Champions

Soft and Chewy Baked Oatmeal

Yields: Makes 6 servings

Ingredients:

- 1 medium-sized apple, grated to 1 cup

- 1 medium-sized apple, sliced

- 1 flax egg (combine 1 Tbs. of ground flax and 3 Tbs. of water)

- 2 ½ cups of rolled oats

- 1 cup of almond milk

- ½ cup of applesauce

- ⅓ cup of dried cranberries

- ¼ cup of melted coconut oil

- 3 Tbs. of molasses

- ½ Tbs. of ground ginger

- 2 tsp. of ground flax

- 1 tsp. of ground cinnamon

- 1 tsp. of vanilla

- ½ tsp. of baking powder

- ½ tsp. of ground ginger

- ¼ tsp. of baking soda

- ¼ tsp. of ground cloves

- A pinch of salt

Method of Preparation:

Start by making the flax egg and set it aside for 5 minutes. Heat up the oven to 350°F and grease an 8" pan.

Take a big bowl and add the rolled oats, ground spices, baking soda, baking powder, ground flax and salt.

Get a separate bowl and mix the flax egg, applesauce, molasses, milk, vanilla and coconut oil.

Combine wet and dry ingredients together; mix until they are well integrated. Fold in the cranberries and grated apple.

Pour into the baking pan and arrange apple slices on top. Bake for about 45 minutes.

Cinnamon Agave Chia Pudding

Yields: Makes 4 servings

Ingredients:

- 2 Tbs. of agave nectar

- 1 tsp. of ground cinnamon

- ½ tsp. of vanilla extract

- ⅛ tsp. of salt

- 2 cups of vanilla almond milk

- ½ cup of chia seeds

Method of Preparation:

Add the almond milk, agave nectar, chia seeds, vanilla, cinnamon and salt in one bowl. Mix until they combine well.

Cover and keep refrigerated for 2 hours before eating. Top with some fresh berries.

Keto-Style Breakfast Hash

Yields: Makes 1 serving

Ingredients:

- 1 large egg

- 1 medium-sized zucchini, diced

- ½ a white onion, chopped

- 2 strips of bacon

- 1 Tbs. of coconut oil or ghee

- 1 Tbs. of parsley or chives, chopped

- ¼ tsp of salt

Method of Preparation:

Cut the bacon into little pieces. In a pan, add the onions and the bacon, letting them brown while stirring often.

Add in the zucchini and let it cook for 15 minutes. When it's done, switch off the heat and add chopped chives or parsley. Fry an egg sunny side up and slide it on top before you start eating.

The Ketogenic-Paleo Breakfast

Yields: Makes 1 serving

Ingredients:

- 2 oz. of wild smoked salmon

- ¼ an avocado, diced

- 2 eggs

- 1 tsp. of ghee

- ½ cup of arugula

- A squeezing of

- A pinch of black pepper

Method of Preparation:

Melt the ghee on a medium heat in a pan. Crack the 2 eggs in and cook them as sunny side ups, which will take about 6 minutes.

In the meantime, toss the arugula and avocado together. Get a plate and put them there.

Arrange the salmon slices on the same plate and squeeze lemon juice on everything. Sprinkle the black pepper at this time.

When the eggs are done, place them on the plate and get ready to dig in!

Pumpkin Chocolate Chip Bread

Yields: Makes 5 servings

Ingredients:

- 3 eggs

- 1 ½ cups of almond flour

- ¼ cup of honey

- ½ cup of small dark chocolate chips (optional)

- ¾ cup of canned pumpkin

- 3 Tbs. of coconut oil

- 1 Tbs. of ground cinnamon

- 2 tsp. of pumpkin pie spice

- 1 tsp. of baking powder

- 1 tsp. of baking soda

- 1 tsp. of vanilla essence or one pod

Method of Preparation:

Mix all the almond flour, ground cinnamon, pie spice, baking powder and baking soda in one bowl.

In a smaller bowl, mix the honey, canned pumpkin, oil, and vanilla essence together.

Pour the contents of the small bowl into the bowl with the dry ingredients and mix until they combine.

Add in the chocolate chips at this point. Get the oven going at 350°F and prep a bread pan by greasing it.

Bake the bread for about 35 to 45 minutes. When it's done, let the bread cool on a rack before eating.

Zucchini Strips Bacon n' Eggs

Yields: Makes 4 servings

Ingredients:

- 4 eggs

- 4 cups of zucchini shreds

- ½ cup of Asiago, Parmesan or Romano cheese, grated

Method of Preparation:

Slice your bacon strips into half and cut them lengthwise into thinner strips.

Get a pan and let the bacon cook for 3 minutes. Toss in the zucchini noodles and season the mix with salt and pepper.

Flatten the mix and create four indents so you can crack the eggs in. Sprinkle on the cheese.

Crack the eggs into a dent each. Let them cook for 3 minutes on a medium-high heat. Cover and allow it to cook for another few minutes before eating, depending on how you like your eggs cooked.

Jalapeno Cheese Waffles

Yields: Makes 2 servings

Ingredients:

- 3 large eggs

- 1 Jalapeno

- 3 oz. of cream cheese

- 3 oz. of cheddar cheese

- 1 Tbs. of coconut flour

- 1 tsp. of psyllium husk powder

- 1 tsp. of baking powder

- Salt and pepper

Method of Preparation:

Using an immersion blender, mix all the ingredients until they become a smooth consistency.

Prep your waffle iron and when it's ready, pour the mixture in. Let it cook for about 6 minutes.

Top it with some cream cheese, avocado slices and tomato salsa, or experiment with toppings of your choice!

Banana Chia Yoghurt

Yields: Makes 1 serving

Ingredients:

- 1 ripe and spotted banana

- 2 Tbs. of grounded chia seeds

- 2 Tbs. of cashews, raw

- ½ cup of almond milk, unsweetened

- A quart of lemon for juice

- A pinch of cinnamon

- A pinch of salt

Method of Preparation:

Start by soaking the chia in 4 tablespoons of almond milk for 20 minutes.

Soak the raw cashews in water for 20 minutes so it softens.

Blend all the ingredients in a high-speed blender or a food processor until they're all smooth.

If you'd like a thinner consistency, add in some more almond milk. Top it with some nuts and dried fruits before devouring!

Cranberry Pecan Honey Muffin

Yields: Makes 12 servings

Ingredients:

- 2 eggs

- 2 ⅛ cup of almond flour

- 1 cup of cranberries

- ½ cup of orange juice

- ½ cup of pecans, chopped

- ⅛ cup of coconut flour

- ¼ cup of honey

- 2 Tbs. of melted coconut oil

- ½ Tbs. orange zest

- 1 tsp. of vanilla

- ½ tsp of baking soda

Method of Preparation:

Start by heating up the oven to a 350°F and line a muffin tray. Set aside.

Take a mixing bowl and combine the eggs, coconut oil, vanilla, orange juice, honey and the zest. Then, add the almond flour, coconut flour and baking soda. Mix (but don't over mix) until it combines.

Use a spoon and stir in the cranberries and pecans. Pour the batter into the muffin tray and press down to ensure they are filled properly. Top them with some cranberries.

Let it bake for about 25 minutes and when the muffins are done, allow them to cool before removing from the tray.

Super Keto Lunches

Roasted Butternut Squash with Applewood Bacon and Kale

Yields: Makes 6 servings

Ingredients:

- 4 applewood bacon strips, cut into small pieces

- 2 bunches of kale, torn

- 2 cups of butternut squash, diced

- ½ cup of pomegranate seeds

- ⅛ cup of salted and roasted pepitas

- ¼ cup of red onion, finely diced

- ¼ cup of apple cider or apple juice

- 5 Tbs. of apple cider vinegar

- 3 Tbs. of maple syrup

- 2 Tbs. of extra virgin olive oil

- 1 Tbs. of lemon juice

- 1 tsp. of Dijon mustard

- Salt and pepper to taste

Method of preparation:

Start by heating up the oven to 400°F and line a baking pan for the squash.

Into this baking pan, pour 1 tablespoon of oil and toss with salt. Roast for 25 minutes while stirring once in a while.

In the meantime, cook the bacon until it becomes crispy. Save 2 tablespoons of the fat.

Use the bacon fat to sauté the onions for about 1 minute. Add maple syrup, cider, mustard, cider vinegar, salt and pepper. Stir so the ingredients integrate and once it starts to boil, reduce heat to a simmer so it cooks for 5 minutes.

Sprinkle salt on the washed kale before adding in the olive oil and lemon juice. Massage the kale until it starts to darken in color and the quantity reduces by half. This should take about 5 minutes.

Toss the kale with a couple of tablespoons of the dressing. Top it with the squash, pomegranate, bacon and pepitas.

Broccoli, Almonds and Feta Lunch Salad

Yields: Makes 4 servings

Ingredients:

- 1 clove of garlic

- 16 oz. of broccoli cut into florets

- ½ cup of slivered almonds

- ½ cup or more of crumbled feta cheese

- 5 Tbs. of extra virgin olive oil

- 2 Tbs. of red wine vinegar

- 1 ¼ tsp of salt

- A pinch of hot pepper flakes

Method of preparation:

In a pot of water, add 1 teaspoon of salt and let water boil. Add in the broccoli florets when the water is boiling and let them cook for 3 minutes. Remove broccoli and set aside to cool.

Take the garlic clove and mash it together with ¼ teaspoon of salt. Add in the pepper flakes and red wine vinegar, letting the ingredients sit for 10 minutes.

Pour 1 tablespoon of olive oil in a frying pan to heat up and fry almonds until they lightly brown, about 2 to 3 minutes. Remove them and move to a plate.

After 10 minutes, whisk in the 4 tablespoons of olive oil into the garlic and vinegar mix. Integrate the feta, broccoli and almonds in a bowl; toss with the dressing. Eat immediately!

Easy Tempeh Sandwich

Yields: Makes 4 to 6 servings

Ingredients:

- ½ a red pepper

- 8 oz. of tempeh block

- 4 Tbs. of homemade guacamole

- 2 Tbs. of spicy mustard

- A pinch of turmeric

- A pinch of salt

- A bunch of leaves of your choice

Method of preparation:

Heat up oven to 375°F and line your baking pan. Cut your tempeh block into half. Then slice each into another half so you get 4 pieces of tempeh.

Sprinkle a pinch of turmeric and salt over the slices and gently rub into the tempeh. Bake the tempeh for 10 minutes.

Once the tempeh cools slightly, start assembling your sandwich by spreading guacamole on two tempeh slices and spicy mustard on the remaining two. Add in the veggies and you're done!

Cheese and Spinach Pesto Muffin

Yields: Makes 10 servings

Ingredients:

- 6 large eggs

- 4.4 oz.

- 1.8 oz. of olives, sliced

- ⅔ cup of fresh spinach

- ¼ cup of sun-dried tomatoes, chopped

- 3 Tbs. of pesto

- Salt and pepper

Method of Preparation:

Heat up your oven to 350°F. Prepare the spinach by blanching it in boiling water for 1 minute, then putting it in a cold water bath to stop the cooking process. Squeeze out all the water before cooking the spinach.

Crack the 6 eggs into a bowl. Whisk in the pesto, salt and pepper until ingredients combine. Take a muffin tray and equally divide the tomatoes, olives and crumbled cheese into each mound. Then pour in the egg mixture and let the muffins bake for about 20 to 25 minutes. Can be stored for up to 5 days in the refrigerator!

Easy Avocado Salmon Sushi

Yields: Makes 48 pieces

Ingredients:

- 1 avocado, sliced

- 4 seaweed paper

- 2 Tbs. of softened butter

- 1 Tbs. of rice vinegar

- 18 oz. of cauliflower, blitzed

- 2 oz. of smoked salmon

- Whipped cream cheese

Method of Preparation:

In a pan on medium heat, add in the cauliflower rice together with butter and sauté for 10 to 15 minutes. Then, let the cauliflowers rest.

Take the seaweed paper and coat it with a thin layer of cream cheese. Pour the rice vinegar into the cauliflower and stir well.

Take some of the rice and pat a thin layer onto the cream cheese. At the bottom edge of the nori, arrange the avocado and salmon. Roll it up and voila, you're having sushi for lunch!

Pizza for the Keto Soul

Yields: Makes 2 servings

Ingredients:

Crust

- 4 Tbs. of almond flour

- 3 Tbs. of coconut flour

- 1 tsp. of oregano

- 1 tsp. of red pepper, crushed

- 1 tsp. of salt

- ½ tsp of fennel seed

- ½ tsp of garlic powder

Toppings

- Pepperoni slices

- 6 oz. of fresh mozzarella, sliced

- 3 Tbs. of ricotta cheese

- 2 Tbs. of jalapenos, sliced

- ½ cup of pizza sauce

Method of Preparation:

Heat up the oven to 400°F. In a small heatproof bowl, melt the cheese until it's soft, not gooey. Pour in the flours and egg, and combine well.

Take the formed dough and place it between 2 parchment papers. Bake it for 12 to 15 minutes. Remove and start assembling the pizza.

Start by layering on the pizza sauce, then the sliced mozzarella, some ricotta, the pepperoni slices and lastly the peppers. Bake for 10 minutes and garnish with some basil before digging in!

Baked Squash and Quiche Boat

Yields: Makes 2 servings

Ingredients:

- 2 large eggs

- 1 small acorn squash, washed and dried

- ¼ cup of fresh tomatoes, diced

- 1 Tbs. of whole milk

- 4 tsp. of Parmesan cheese

- 2 ½ tsp. of freshly chopped chives

- ½ tsp. of freshly cracked black pepper

- ½ tsp. of sea salt

Method of Preparation:

Heat up the oven to 375°F and prepare the squash by cutting it into half lengthwise and removing all its seeds. At the bottom of both the squash halves, cut a little bit off so they are able to stand.

Take a baking pan and put the squash halves on it with the flesh side down. Fill the tray with water about ¼ of the squash is filled. Cover the baking pan with tin foil loosely and let it bake for about 25 minutes.

Take the squash out and let it cool for 5 minutes. Turn up the oven to 400°F. Take out the squash from the pan and pour out the water, leaving a thin layer left. Put the squash back, with the flesh side up this time. Season with half of the salt and half of the pepper on the squash.

Take a bowl and whisk in the eggs with the milk until combined. Season with the rest of the salt and pepper, and add in the chives.

Add half of the tomatoes in the center of one squash and the second half on the other squash. Slowly pour the egg mix into the squashes, filling them up until it just reaches the top.

Cover the dish with tin foil and bake for 25 to 35 minutes. The eggs are supposed to be just set. Right before it's done, remove and sprinkle the cheese on it. Bake again for 5 more minutes. Dig in!

Fig and Blue Cheese Walnut Salad

Yields: Makes 2 servings

Ingredients:

Dressing

- 3 Tbs. of fig preserves

- 1to 2 Tbs. of water

- 1 tsp. of balsamic vinegar

Salad

- 5 bacon strips, roughly chopped and cooked

- 4 oz. of salad greens like watercress, arugula or any of your choice

- 4 fresh figs

- Blue cheese, crumbled

- ½ cup of walnuts, toasted and chopped roughly

Method of Preparation:

Take a microwave-safe bowl and mix fig preserves with water. Put it for 10 seconds in the microwave at intervals and to warm the dressing properly. Stir in the balsamic vinegar and adjust to desired taste.

When it's time to assemble, add the walnuts and bacons while still warm onto the bed of leaves. Add in the figs and crumble the blue cheese. Add on the dressing while still warm and toss until evenly distributed.

Italian Cabbage Rolls

Yields: Makes 3 servings

Ingredients:

- 16 oz. of good quality ground beef

- 2 eggs

- 1 cabbage head

- ½ cup of coconut cream

- ¼ cup of psyllium husk powder or chia seed flour

- ¼ Tbs. of red chili flakes

- 1 tsp. of mixed herbs

- 1 tsp. of sea salt

- Bit of cooking fat like coconut oil, lard or ghee)

- Ground black pepper

Method of Preparation:

Start heating up the oven to 350°F. Get a pot and boil a quart of water with a pinch of salt.

Put 6 leaves into the water and let it cook for 5 minutes.

Remove the leaves and set them on a plate to cool down. Get started on the stuffing by mixing the room-temperature ground beef with the eggs, flour, coconut cream, mixed herbs, some chili flakes and a good pinch of black pepper. Mix until everything is blended well.

Lay out one cabbage leave on a cutting board and put a scoop of the filling on it. Press it down into an oval shape and wrap the leaf tightly.

Make as many rolls and keep the sizes same so the cabbage cooks evenly.

Grease a Pyrex dish with fat and put the cabbage rolls, filling up the space. Bake for 45 minutes.

High Fat, Low Carb Dinner Ideas

Couscous with Sundried Tomatoes and Grapeseed Oil

Yields: Makes 1 serving

Ingredients:

- 4 cups of cauliflower couscous

- 1 cup of leeks, thinly sliced

- 1 cup of sundried tomatoes

- 2 garlic cloves, minced

- 1 Tbs. of grapeseed oil

- Sea salt and black pepper to taste

Method of Preparation:

Put sundried tomatoes in a bowl of water to get them rehydrated again.

To make cauliflower couscous, pulse the florets until it's a fine texture.

Sauté the leeks and garlic in grapeseed oil on low heat for a couple of minutes. In the meantime, chop up the hydrated tomatoes and add it into the pan. Keep cooking until the leeks are soft.

Add in the cauliflower and cook it until it's softened. Be sure to not cook too long or it will turn into mush. Season with salt and pepper before eating!

Lamb and Buttered Fennel

Yields: Makes 1 serving

Ingredients:

- 4 oz. of lamb stew meat, cut into 1 inch cubes

- 3.5 oz. of fennel bulb, sliced

- 1 oz. of onion, sliced round

- 3 Tbs. of butter

- ¼ cup of water

- Salt and pepper

Method of Preparation:

Start by stirring the lamb and the onions in a broiler pan for about 6 minutes. Place the meat under broiler on high for about 6 minutes. Cook until the meat is pink inside, or if you prefer it thoroughly cooked then leave it on longer.

Season the meat with salt and pepper. Get a skillet and melt the butter in. Sauté the fennel for a few minutes and add a pinch of salt. Pour in water and cover the skillet with a lid.

Let it cook for 10 more minutes and serve together with the lamb for your dinner!

Carbonara and Roasted Cabbage

Yields: Makes 4 servings

Ingredients:

- 1 green cabbage

- 2 eggs, pastured

- 8 strips of bacon, uncured

- 4 cloves of garlic

- Carbonara sauce

- 1 cup of coconut cream

- ¼ cup of olive oil

- Salt and pepper to taste

Method of preparation:

Preheat oven to 350°F. Trim the bottom of the cabbage and take out the leaves. Slice the leaves to ½ inch slices and lay it down on a cookie sheet that's been oiled.

In a food processor or a pestle and mortar, combine the garlic cloves (skin off), olive oil and salt until they become a paste.

Brush/spread the paste onto the cabbage slices. Bake the cabbage in the oven for 30 minutes. Turn the slices once after 15 minutes and brush it with oil.

Chop the bacon into 1-inch pieces and fry them until they are crispy.

Take a bowl and whisk eggs, coconut cream, melted butter, salt and lots of pepper till it becomes a cream consistency.

The readied cabbage will have a caramelized look. Toss it in the carbonara sauce with the bacon to complete your dinner.

Shrimp n' Vegetables Vindaloo Style
Yields: Makes 2 servings

Ingredients:

- 8 oz. of peeled and deveined prawns

- 1 carrot, chopped finely

- 3 cloves of garlic, minced

- ½ a broccoli head, cut into florets

- ½ a bunch of kale, chopped roughly

- ½ a bunch of collard greens, chopped roughly

- ½ a red onion, sliced thinly

- 2 Tbs. of extra virgin olive oil

- 1 Tbs. of vindaloo seasoning

- Salt and pepper

Method of Preparation:

Season prawns with vindaloo seasoning. Heat a skillet with 1 tablespoon of oil and sear one side of the prawns for 3 minutes. Sear the second side for 2 minutes. Take the shrimp off the heat and cover.

Add 1 more tablespoon of the oil and sauté with the carrots for about 5 minutes. Then, toss in the broccoli and garlic, cooking it for another 3 minutes. Season with salt and pepper.

Then, put the chopped greens and some vindaloo seasoning in and sauté for about 2 to 3 minutes.

Toss the shrimps in with the greens and eat while it's still hot!

Salmon Whiskey Glaze and Mango Chutney

Yields: Makes 2 servings

Ingredients:

- Salmon

- 2 fillets of salmon

- 1 Tbs. of soy sauce

- 1 Tbs. of brown sugar

- 2 tsp. of Dijon mustard

- ½ cup of whiskey

- Chutney

- 8 oz. of mango, diced

- 2 Tbs. of fresh cilantro, minced

- 1 tomato, diced and seeded

- 2 habanero peppers, deseeded and chopped

- ½ tsp. of salt

Method of Preparation:

Heat up the oven to 400°F. Take a pan and add in the whiskey, brown sugar, soy sauce and mustard.

Whisk the ingredients and put it on a low heat until it comes to a slow bubble. Whisk every now and then throughout 7 to 8 minutes. When the sauce is reduced and thickened, remove from the heat.

Place a skillet on medium-high heat until the oil is hot. In the meantime, season salmon with salt and put them on the skillet, skin-side down. Let each salmon cook on each side for 3 to 4 minutes. When it's brown, take it off the heat and brush the glaze on. Put it in the oven for 5 minutes.

Brush once with the glaze before serving and top with the mango chutney. Place the salmon on a bed of greens (your choice) seasoned with some lemon juice and olive oil.

White "Tom Yam" with Shrimp and Chicken

Yields: Makes 2 servings

Ingredients:

Broth

- 4 cups of chicken broth

- 1 ½ cup of coconut milk, full fat

- 1 cup of fresh cilantro

- 3 kaffir lime leaves (substitute with zest of 1 lime if cannot find)

- 1 inch of fresh lemongrass, sliced

- 1 inch of fresh galangal root or 3 pieces of dried galangal root

- 4 dried Thai Bird's Eye chili, or one jalapeno

- Salt to taste

Soup

- 3.5 oz. of shrimp of chicken meat

- 30 grams of oyster mushrooms or any kind, sliced

- 30 grams of red onions, sliced

- 1 Tbs. of fish sauce

- 1 Tbs. of coconut oil

- 1 lime

Method of Preparation:

To make the broth, start by putting all ingredients in a pan and bring them to a simmer for 20 minutes. Strain out the ingredients and pour the broth back into the pan.

Add in the meat of your choice with the fish sauce into the broth. Slide in the onions and mushrooms.

Let everything simmer for 10 minutes or until meat is cooked.

Squeeze the juice out of 1 lime and your tom yam soup is ready!

Pan Seared Tuna with Vietnamese Salad

Yields: Makes 2 servings

Ingredients:

- 2 pieces of 6 oz. tuna steak

- 4 cups of Napa cabbage, thinly sliced

- 1 cup of cucumber, thinly sliced

- ½ cup of carrots, cut to matchsticks

- ⅓ cup of red onion, sliced

- 1 orange, sectioned out and chopped

- 2 Tbs. of rice vinegar

- 2 Tbs. of fresh lime juice

- 2 Tbs. of fresh cilantro, chopped

- 1 Tbs. of sugar

- ½ tsp. of dark sesame oil

- ¼ tsp. of sambal oelek or Sriracha

- Salt and pepper

- Butter or ghee

Method of Preparation:

Get a grill pan and put it on a medium-high heat. Season the fillets with salt and pepper. Melt a bit of butter/ghee and put the fish, cooking it for 2 minutes each sides.

In a big bowl, toss the cabbage with onions, carrots, cucumber and orange. Add the sugar, rice vinegar, sesame oil, sambal, cilantro and lime juice in a small bowl. Whisk until they integrate well.

Keep 1 tablespoon of the dressing aside and drizzle the rest onto the salad. Toss them well. Cut the tuna into ¼ inch thick pieces. Divide the salad onto two plates and gently place the tuna steaks on each plate.

Drizzle remaining dressing and get ready to eat!

Rosemary and Maple Syrup Pork Chops

Yields: Makes 2 servings

Ingredients:

- Pork Chop

- 4 pieces of pork chop

- ½ an apple, sliced

- 2 Tbs. of olive oil

- Salt, pepper and paprika to taste

- 4 good sprigs of rosemary

- Vinaigrette

- 2 Tbs. of apple cider vinegar

- 2 Tbs. of olive oil

- 1 Tbs. of lemon juice

- 1 Tbs. of maple syrup

- Salt and pepper

Method of Preparation:

Get an iron skillet and heat it up in an oven set to 400°F. Prep the chops by patting them dry with a paper towel.

Rub them with olive oil and season according to taste. Get the skillet out and adjust the stove's heat to high. Sear the pork chops for 2 minutes on each side.

Arrange apple slices and the rosemary sprigs on the chops. Put it in the oven for 10 minutes to complete cooking process.

As the pork chops cook, make the apple cider vinaigrette by whisking all the ingredients, adding the oil last. Pour the oil slowly as you whisk so it emulsifies.

Once the pork chops are done, plate it, pour the vinaigrette on top and enjoy!

Green Pea Lemon Fraiche Soup

Yields: Makes 3 servings

Ingredients:

- 56 oz. of fresh peas

- 4 oz. of cream fraiche

- ½ cup of salt (or lesser)

- ½ cup of sugar

- ½ cup of water

- 3 quarts of water

- 1 Tbs. lemon juice + zest of 1 lemon

Method of Preparation:

In a large pot, mix 3 quarts of water, sugar and salt. Bring to boil and add half of the peas to cook between 6 to 8 minutes. When the peas are done, dunk them in a bowl of water and ice using a colander or a skimmer. Repeat same process with remaining peas.

Add the cooked peas into a food processor or blender. Pour in ½ a cup of water and blend until smooth. If needed, use a fine meshed sieve and pass the peas through them.

Mix the cream fraiche with lemon juice and zest. Drizzle the soup with some olive oil and serve with the crème fraiche.

The Ketogenic Diet: The Origins and Future

'There is a lot of misinformation and disinformation—if not outright, unwarranted hysteria—concerning the potential risks of a low-carbohydrate, fat-based, ketogenic diet. Some of this popularized hysteria borders on the absurd.' –
Nora Gedgaudas

The Ketogenic diet, unlike most of today's weight-loss fads, was not a diet plan birthed out of desperation to lose weight quickly and noticeably. In fact, it wasn't even developed in this era – which is a good thing, in case you were beginning to think that the diets of the generation of 'instant gratification' would ever be anything worth deliberating on.

No; the Ketogenic Diet is much more than a quick crash-diet plan to help you fit into your wedding dress. Unlike it's predecessors and successors alike, it is a well researched, scientific dietary plan that began it's illustrious claim to fame not as a weight loss initiative, but rather as a food-plan, designed by Dr. Russell Wilder of Mayo Clinic, in 1924 to effectively treat epilepsy, most famously used by the Hollywood's own Abraham's family for their then five-year-old son.

This diet is still extremely famous in Hollywood but for very different reasons – today, the Keto-diet has been brought back into the limelight as a healthy alternative to the massively unhealthy lifestyles of the rich and famous, such as juicing or any of the millions of other fad diets that are introduced every other week.

If you are still on the fence about those diets, however, allow me to explain why the Keto-diet is superior.

To start, the Keto diet works on one simple principal – in order to burn fat, one must consume fat. It allows for your body to be able to effectively partake in normal meals and foods. The reasoning behind this is quite simple – the Keto-Diet differentiates quite clearly between body-fat and body-weight, and in doing so the diet targets more than water weight or muscle weight the way the fad diets do. Instead, the Keto diet focuses on ensuring that any weight you do lose is 'real weight'.

Think of it like this – the human body derives energy from one of three sources – carbohydrates, fats and proteins. Generally, we tend to use glucose, which we gain from burning carbohydrates; however, a better alternative to glucose is the metabolized beta-hydroxybutric acid, which we get from burning fat. Because of the way that the Keto diet is designed to work, the body begins to adapt to a new status quo – one where instead of looking for carbs to break down so it can get a quick energy fix, it instead burns fat. In doing so, as a residue of sorts, it floods the body with higher ketone bodies in the blood, a phenomenon also known as Ketosis.

The simple science behind this diet is that with a specific high fat diet, the liver, which is producing these ketone bodies, allows them to be used as an alternative source of energy. To put it in layman's terms – it creates a loophole in the body, where one can intake fat and burn it almost instantly.

Ketones are basically fat breakdown products that therefore stand to replace the role of glucose as the major fuel of most organs inside the human body and most notably the brain! It doesn't end there though – the beauty of Ketosis is that this particular transition has been scientifically proven to simultaneously act as a non-toxic, non-medicated prevention for diseases ranging from epilepsy to cancer! We'll elaborate on these particular health benefits later on, in Chapter Two and Chapter Three, when we talk about who is best suited to use the Ketogenic Diet and which particular diet, or rather which particular variation of the diet, would suit you best.
For now, we just want to give you an overview of how the diet came about so that you have a clear understanding of it's scientific roots, as well as the potential it holds to become the ultimate lifestyle choice for the health-conscious.

Keto-Diets – Targets and Types

"A low-carb, ketogenic diet needs to be high in fat, not protein, to produce adequate ketones." –
Jimmy Moore

The first rule that one must adhere to as they embark on the path of Ketogenic Weight Loss is that in order for the diet to work, there must be a consistent state of ketosis. Ketosis is that state in which your body is tricked into burning fat for energy instead of glucose. The way one ensures that this happens is by, of course, resorting to a limited carbohydrate intake so that you body has no choice *but* burn fat.

This is where you are going to have to take a massive leap of faith though. Remember, this is a scientifically researched diet plan, not some weird teen fad, so, even if it does sound insane, keep an open mind.

For all your life, when you've heard the word 'diet' you've probably associated it with steering clear of all those nasty fat rich foods that beckon to you at midnight for that one last bite. I'm not going to say that all of that is wrong –what I am going to say is there is more to the picture.

Fat, just like proteins or carbohydrates, are in fact part and parcel of a healthy human diet – why does it turn into this gluttonous monster that starts padding us with blubber in all the wrong places?

Well, maybe because we are stocking up on it, but we're also forgetting to use it properly. It's kind of like at Christmas when you buy all those stocking stuffers, which are absolutely fabulous as stocking stuffers, but God forbid that you accidentally forget where you put them, or somehow don't get around to sending them out, because the very next morning all your precious little token gifts somehow morph into these cheap little boxes that nobody has any use for – those clutter-some gifts, which only yesterday were so promising and full of potential.

Basically, your fat is like your cutesy holiday stocking stuffer—great if you unwrap it in time, or rather burn it in time, but if not it is just a bunch of clutter and waste that tends to build and build.

Now that we have established the way the Keto diet works inside your body, let's talk about the external aspects, or rather let's talk about one specific external factor – your intake.

What Should I Put in My Body?

When you are on the Keto diet, the answer is relatively simple; avoid carbs and sugars and you should be good to go. We'll take you through specific meal planes later on in the book but generally speaking that is the rule of thumb.

On a more micro-level, however, the diet can vary, which is why we'll be expounding first on the four most popular variations of the diet before we go into what components each diet specifically includes.

The Classic Keto Diet

General Overview of the Classic Diet

The classic Keto diet is, of course, a throwback to its scientific roots and generally requires the involvement of a licensed dietician. They will first evaluate the individual's age, weight, and physical activity against their cultural food preferences before making a dietary recommendation.

However, the diet is basically drawn up in terms of a rigid mathematical ratio, where the fat to carbohydrate ratio is required to be at a 4:1, 3:1 or 2:1. It is common for kids to be prescribed a 4:1 ration, as the energy requirement for children is generally about 20% less than the recommended daily amounts. This may change based on your child's weight, but it is unlikely there will be much variation.

What Does It Contain?

The basic food module of the classic diet generally consists of heavy creams, proteins, and very low carbohydrate based vegetables. It is also common to use pure fat forms, such as butter or vegetable oils, as part of the plan.

It is noteworthy to mention that the classic diet is far from a balanced 'lifestyle diet;' it has very little in the way of calcium sources or many other basic vegetable or fruit based vitamins, which is why the diet requires mandatory supplements.

Who Does This Diet Help?

Traditionally the classic Keto diet is used for children with control seizures; recent studies have shown that this diet, in specific control groups, has proven to be more effective than seizure medication therapy.

The Medium-Chain Triglyceride (MCT) Variant

General Overview of the MCT Keto-Diet

The MCT Diet is a variation on the Keto-diet, which is generally considered to be a more lax variant. 'MCT' refers basically to a specific type of oil – MCT oils in contrast to LCT oils are known for producing ketones more easily – which is what ultimately what allows for the followers of this particular diet to indulge in more carbohydrates and proteins while on this Diet plan.

What Does It Contain?

The basic food module of the MCT Diet is a 1:1 ratio; this is what makes this version of the diet so much more adult friendly. Not only are you allowed greater variety in the components of the diet, but you are also allowed greater portions, which can make it easier for many adults to stick to the MCT instead of the classic.

Who Does This Diet Help?

The MCT variation of the Keto diet is more adjacent with those of you who are interested in the weight-loss aspect of the Keto diet. Not only is the diet easier to follow than the classic, but it is also easier to maintain as a lifestyle choice, which is critical for long-term diets.

The Low Glycemic Index Treatment (LGIT)

General Overview of the LGIT Diet

Technically speaking, the LGIT is not a variant of the Keto diet like the MCT, but rather a 'similar' high-fat diet. For all intents and purposes though the diet is as good as a variant – it is used to treat seizures, and focuses on the same low carbohydrate, low glycemic index – the only major difference is that unlike the Keto-diet the LGIT does not intend to put the boy into a state of ketosis, and as such is less likely to induce manifestations of low blood-sugar or nausea.

What Does It Contain?

The basic food module of the LGIT diet is based on the glycemic index – the diet restricts carbohydrates, which are higher than a 50 on the glycemic index. But despite the restrictions the LGIT is far easier to follow as an adult – the fact that it measures in portion sizes as opposed to grams let's you eat out at restaurants or go on trips, you just have to put a little more planning into your outings

Who Does This Diet Help?

LGIT is known to work well for children and adults –however, the diet is required to have physician supervision, like the classic Keto diet. Adults on this diet have reported favorable weight loss; however, it is critical those follow-ups are scheduled monthly, since the diet aims to reduce seizures and weight by careful control of the blood glucose levels – remember, this is all about healthy living.

The Modified Atkins Diet (MAD)

General Overview of the Modified Atkins Diet

Much like the LGIT, the modified Atkins diet isn't really a Keto diet at all – the original Atkin's diet itself was actually a very well known weight-loss diet, developed on the basis of a very low carbohydrate intake (like we said, fat isn't your enemy carbs are!). The modified version is basically the Aktin's way of acknowledging that the low carb intake needs to be balanced out by a higher intake of fat foods – and was developed at the John Hopkin's Hospital as a 1:1 balance ratio of fat to carbs and proteins.

What Does It Contain?

The modified Atkins diet is possibly the easiest of Keto or Keto-like diets; for one, the diet has zero dietary restrictions in terms of calories or fluids – all you have to do is limit your carb intake to about 15 grams a day. In fact, the diet is so lenient that breakfasts on the Atkins diet can range from bacon and ham to cheese omelets – all topped off with healthy servings on butter on your non-grain based bread. There is a bit of a restriction on your fruit intake as well, but that is mainly because of the carbohydrate count; low-carb vegetables are fine and make great additions to your meal.

Who Does This Diet Help?

The modified Atkin's diet is a great way to ease yourself or your family into Keto diets, mainly because it is so lax with the carb intake, which is generally considered the most difficult part of maintaining a Ketogenic diet.

All in all, if you intend of starting your Keto-journey from the comfort of your home, you had best focus on the LGIT of the modified Atkins; both are individualized diet plans but are widely considered to be less rigid than the classic Ketogenic diet, which, like the MCT diet, is best started only after a detailed consultation with your doctor!

How to Start and Maintain the Keto Diet

"Some organs in your body prefer using these ketones instead of glucose for fuel when they are available, like the heart." – Sarah Banks

They say the journey of a thousand miles starts with the first step. Similarly, the journey of a Keto diet starts before the actual start of the diet. In fact, it is essentially imperative if you want to follow the three golden P's that you launch into your Keto diet long before you actually begin your diet.

You do know what the 3 Golden P's are, right?

No?

They are simple - Plan, Pursue, and Persevere, in exactly that order.

Many people tend to jump into the Keto diets on a whim; they tend to perceive it to be a fad diet and treat it as such – what you need to understand is that the Keto diets are nothing like regular diets. They are not something you can just jump into or jump out of –your body *must* be eased into a state of ketosis just as it must be eased out of it – anything else will not only risk nullifying any and all effects of your diet, but it will also risk you and your health.

The Keto diet, despite its name, is more of a lifestyle sense. This is why it is so important to 'Plan' for it before your choose to pursue it. Think very carefully about the circumstantial situations you may find yourself in, and ask yourself how you would deal with what were previously regular events, like a night out with your friend or a fancy dinner with your significant other.

Trust us, it is a lot harder than it seems. That is why in order for you to get the most out of your Keto diet, you are going to have to establish it in slow and steady steps, by doing things like cutting down on your carbohydrate intake over the span of a few months, cutting your carb intake down to 10 grams is not something you are going to be able to do all on a sudden, and even if by some miracle you do – you won't be able to maintain it. Some people find it easier if they start by creating 'mini-ketosis' inductions before the diet, where they combine and exercise and food habits to induce a period of ketosis.

Additionally, there are certain supplements you are going to need as well as certain adjustments you are going to have to make to your daily exercise regimen, or way of living – all in all, you are going to have to sit down, and seriously plan out how you are going to adapt your lifestyle to the diet –and start easing yourself into all of the changes before you embark on your true Keto-Diet journey. Once you've planned out your life on the Keto diet, your next job is to start pursuing it.

So your next step is quite literally to start the diet – I know that can sound super redundant, but the truth is it is easy to lull yourself into a sense of false security, where you think you are doing something close enough. There is no such thing as close enough; put on your grown-up pants because this is where things start getting rough.

In order for you to properly follow or rather pursue your Keto diet, you are going to have to start by measuring your blood ketones levels. You are going to want to target 1.5-3 mmol/L – although initially you may find it hard to get beyond the 0.5-1.5 mmol/L plateau – this is no reason to be discouraged, the latter is still a state of ketosis, it is merely too mild for you to actually be getting any visible effects in terms of your body weight. These blood ketones can be easily measured at home with many of the gadgets that are available over the counter and can even be tested with urine tests if you're not a fan of pricking your finger on a regular basis.

As previously stated, pursuing your diet is going to be much harder than just planning for it, especially as you are forced to adapt to regular day-to-day life. Which brings us to our final part of the process – perseverance.

The Keto diet, is not something you can just go on and come off of when the mood strikes; there are actual physical ramifications to you cutting out carbs and adding them back in to your diet plan. This is why, although it is understandable that you won't stay on the Keto diet indefinitely, it is strongly suggested that you remember to ease out of it – side-effects to this diet includes insulin resistance, once the carbohydrates are reintroduced. For these reasons, when you choose to come off a Keto diet it is important to start by building up to regular carbohydrate portions, as well as offsetting it through regular exercise so that your body is less likely to induce gastric shock or weight gain.

Keto-Diet FAQ's for Parents

"Newborn babies who are exclusively breastfed will go into a state of ketosis within twelve hours of birth, and ketones provide about 25 percent of their energy needs." – Eric C. Westman

While the Ketogenic diet can be difficult for adults, it can be even harder for children, and that means it is absolutely the hardest for parents. Because of it's massive success in relieving or at least showing substantial improvement for children who suffer from epilepsy and similar chronic seizures, the diet is a popular choice amongst parents who want to try a non-medicated seizure prevention method.

That is of course until your child starts to crave ice cream or McDonald's like all the 'other' kids. This chapter is exclusively dedicated to those parents who have to deal with a child on the Keto diet, so that you can find great alternatives to your child's cravings and, more importantly, understand all the nitty-gritty details of how the diet is keeping your child free of all those pesky seizures.

I'm sure you have about a million questions as a Keto-Parent, or a prospective Keto-Parent. This is where you find your answers.
Ready?
Here we go!

1. *Why am I feeding my child all these fats; won't that just make them gain weight?*

- To make this simple – no.
  Your child is not randomly walking around eating tons of greasy bacon and mountains of clotted cream – they are on a scientifically generated mathematical formula that carefully calculates the amount of fat that your child needs to consume to balance out their

carbohydrate and protein intake so that their bodies can switch into a state of ketosis. If you feel like you are seeing any abnormal weight gain, consult a doctor immediately so they can ensure this is merely the regular weight gain associated with 'child-growth.'

2. *With such strictly regulated portions, won't m child be hungry all the time?*

- Ketosis has a tendency to suppress regular appetites – so if your child is already on the Keto diet they likely won't be as hungry as normal kids anyway. Most of their hunger pangs are going to be habitual – so during the first few weeks, they may indeed feel a bit off, but the longer they are on the diet, the more quickly their body adjusts to the new portions and the ketosis.

3. *How can I take my child out for regular family outings?*

- Regular family outings are not a problem when it comes to Keto diets provided you plan ahead. This is what we meant when we emphasized on planning in the previous chapter. If you want to go on a trip, or a even something as simple as a night out with the family, make sure you ensure that you have either packed something they can eat, or that the restaurant you are going to can provide a Ketogenic meal. Usually, if you explain your situation and ask for your meal to be heated at the restaurant, they'll simply serve it up with everyone else so your child can feel just as normal as everyone else. Remember – it's all about the planning!

Ketogenic diets for children are admittedly difficult when you first begin, but they only have to remain so if you want them to – working on suitable alternatives adaptations is how you keep your child happy, healthy, and, most importantly, seizure free!

Quick and Easy Keto-Diet Recipes

"Carbohydrate overconsumption has created the walking dead." – Stephanie Person

The first four chapters of this book have dealt almost exclusively with the effects and after-effects of the Keto diet – we have discussed the major areas in need of consideration prior to embarking on this journey, as well as the multi-faceted circumstantial situations that you may find yourself in because of the diet.

It is safe to say that you now know exactly what the Keto diet is all about, meaning all you now need is a handful of Keto recipes to tide you over, and we, of course, are about to provide you with just that. Keep in mind that each of these recipes can and should be adapted to suit whichever specific diet form you have chosen for yourself – think of them as changeable options rather than strict recipes, and you'll find yourself with a nice variety of recipes for your daily meals.

Breakfast

Breakfast on the Ketogenic diet can be especially tricky for people who are used to ready-made, processed carbohydrate-based breakfasts, such as cereal, bagels or donuts.

The thing you need to focus on is figuring out substitutes for the main carbohydrate here – flour. Generally, great alternatives are almond flour and coconut flour, but recently Psyllium husk powder has also garnered massive momentum. For instance, the basic batter is now going to be your breakfast staple – while you build everything else around it.

1. The Basic Keto- Waffle/Pancake/ Donut Batter

¼ Cup of **Coconut Flour** (double for **Almond Flour**)

2 Large **Eggs** (Organic)

½ Cup of **Almond Milk**

2 Tablespoons of **Ghee** (can alternate with **Coconut Oil** or **Butter**)

½ Teaspoon of **Cinnamon/Vanilla Extract**

½ Teaspoon **Cream of Tartar**

¼ Teaspoon **Baking Soda**

Stevia Extract - (as needed)

Quick Fixes

The basic batter recipe can be spruced up by a simple helping of fruits and yogurt, or even a topping of whipped cream or butter – but that is just for the easy days; if you really want to get inventive, try adding in jalapeño and cream cheese, and top it off with avocado slices.

Want something even more savory?

Try making a regular waffle, and smother it in home-made pizza sauce (tomato puree, thyme and oregano), and then melt two whole slices of cheese on it while you top it all off with slightly butter fried ham or bacon!

2. The Basic Keto- Omelet

2 Large **Eggs** (Organic)

Salt and Pepper - (as needed)

Quick Fixes

The basic Keto omelet recipe is so basic that you can literally turn this into anything you want. A great option is to pour in all the left over veggies/curry you can find and just turn it into this strange all egg stir-fry –or if you want it to be a little more breakfast-y, just put in a bit of cheese, bacon, and a tomato, and you will have a great bacon and cheese omelets, with the tomatoes giving it a great balance.

3. The Basic Keto- Shake

¼ Cup of **Coconut Milk**

1 Cup of **Almond Milk**

½ Teaspoon of **Vanilla Extract**

½ Cup of **Whey Protein**

1 Tablespoon of **Chia Seeds**

Stevia Extract - (as needed)

Quick Fixes

Generally, the Keto-Shake is more than enough to power you through a morning or even a lunch sometimes. If you're really on the go, it can use some sprucing up at times, so feel free to add all sorts of things to your Shake.

Berries make a great addition for the summer time, while if you're in the mood for it you can actually add in a bit of nutmeg and cinnamon for a more autumn feel. Another quick add in is chocolate, or a bit of instant coffee – it leaves you feeling like you have something that you can sip a bit more slowly, as you go about.

4. Keto-Casseroles

1 Cup of diced **Jalapenos and Tomatoes**

1 Lb. of **Ground Beef**

½ Cup of **Almond Flour**

3 Cups of **Cauliflower**

½ Teaspoon of **Garlic Powder**

½ Teaspoon of **Onion Powder**

1 Teaspoon of **Tomato Paste**

1 Teaspoon of **Dijon Mustard**

3 Large **Eggs**

4 oz. **Cheddar Cheese**

1 Tablespoon **Mayonnaise**

Salt and **Pepper** to Taste

Quick Fixes

Generally, Keto recipes are almost already half made. The Keto-Casserole is going to take a little more time and preparation. Start with the Cauliflower, and rice it with a food processor. Then right before you pour the cauliflower into a bowel add in all other dry ingredients. Then repeat the same process with the ground beef, eggs, mustard, mayonnaise, and tomato paste. Add chees and mix both bowls together till mixture is paste-like. Allow to sit for five minutes, and then transfer to a 9x9baking pan lined with parchment paper. Top with remaining cheese crumbs and bake for 30 minutes at 350F.

And Voila!

Now you have four easily alterable recipes to tide you through an entire week of Keto dieting, all on a pocket-friendly budget. Now it's really all up to you – are you read to change your life as you know it? Start now, plan now, and remember: procrastination is the vice of cowards!

Conclusion

Achieving the weight and body figure that you have long desired is easier with the Ketogenic Diet. I hope that through this book you are able to understand that you don't have to skip meals or starve yourself in order to lose weight; instead, you just have to be smart, and watch what you eat!

Many have proven that this high-fat, low-carb diet is one effective way to shed off the unwanted pounds, plus enjoy a few more health benefits that the Ketogenic Diet includes. My wish is that you will be able to utilize the recipes in this book and use them as you plan your meals for the diet.

Having a healthier lifestyle and following the diet will be a challenge at first, especially when you're not yet used to counting calories and monitoring your body's state, but it will surely be worth it when you see the numbers on the scale decreasing.

Don't waste another day on your old, unhealthy diet; start the Ketogenic Diet today!

Important Message

Finally, my important message to you, as my token of appreciate for downloading my book I've included 3 other books I've written on Ketogenic and added more recipes in this book if you didn't noticed. I greatly appreciate it! Out of all the books available on Ketogenic you've purchased mine.

Thank You and Good Luck! - Karen Taylor

30976625R00099

Made in the USA
San Bernardino, CA
27 February 2016